CENTRAL AMERICA

Edward Parker

MACDONALD YOUNG BOOKS

500339578

First published in 1999 by Macdonald Young Books
An imprint of Wayland Publishers Ltd
© Macdonald Young Books 1999

Macdonald Young Books
61 Western Road
Hove
East Sussex
BN3 1JD

Find Macdonald Young Books on the Internet at
http://www.myb.co.uk

Design and typesetting Roger Kohn Designs
Commissioning editor Rosie Nixon
Editor Merle Thompson
Picture research Gina Brown
Maps János Márffy

We are grateful to the following for permission
to reproduce photographs:
Front Cover: Robert Harding, above (Christopher Rennie);
Robert Harding, below (James Strachan);
Sylvia Corday, page 22; Greg Evans, pages 25, 36 (Greg
Balfour Evans); Eye Ubiquitous, page 41 (Tim Page); Robert
Harding, page 11 above (Gavin Hellier); James Davis Travel,
pages 9, 23, 28, 37 below, 45; Panos, pages 12 above
(Paul Smith), 12/13 below (Sean Sprague), 32 (Tina Gue);
Popperfoto, page 27; South American Pictures, pages 16
(Chris Sharp), 17 (Robert Francis), 19 T Morrison), 24 (Robert
Francis), 30 (T Morrison), 33 (Robert Francis), 34/35
(T Morrison), 35 above (Chris Sharp), 37 above (Chris Sharp),
38/39 (P Dixon), 44 (Robert Francis); Still Pictures, pages 11
below (Nigel Dickinson), 14 (Nigel Dickinson), 15 (Nigel
Dickinson), 26 (Jorgen Schytte), 29 (Heine Pedersen), 31
(Julio Etchart), 39 above (Nigel Dickinson), 40 (Nigel
Dickinson), 43 (Y J Rey-Millet); Tony Stone, pages 8/9
(Will & Den McIntyre), 10 (Hilarie Kavanagh), 20 (Margaret
Gowan), 21 Suzanne Murphy), 42 (Simeone Huber); Trip, page
18 (Robert Belbin).

The statistics given in this book are the most up to date available
at the time of going to press

Printed in Hong Kong by Wing King Tong

A CIP catalogue record for this book is available from
the British Library

ISBN: 0 7500 2620 0

CONTENTS

Words that are explained in the glossary are printed in
SMALL CAPITALS the first time they are mentioned in the text.

INTRODUCTION

Central America is made up of seven countries: Belize, Costa Rica, El Salvador, Honduras, Guatemala, Nicaragua, and Panama. Together, they cover an area of 523,160 square kilometres; twice the size of the UK or of the state of Colorado in the USA. The total population of the region is around 35 million.

These central American nations are well known for their scenic landscapes with, for example, active volcanoes, steamy TROPICAL forests or attractive Caribbean coasts. Some of them are famous for the ruins of magnificent cities and temples built by the Mayan Indians. Many Indians, with their distinctive colourful cultures, still live in the region.

Today, however, many members of Central American society are facing harsh realities, such as extreme poverty and violent crime.

Before the first Europeans arrived, the region was home to millions of Indians. The most famous of the civilizations that developed here was that of the Mayas, which flourished between 1,000 and 2,000 years ago. The Mayan empire was very large and included most of Guatemala and Belize, western Honduras and a large part of southern Mexico. The Mayas built temples with towers over 60 metres high, and constructed magnificent cities, like Tikal, in Guatemala, which covers 16 square kilometres. There were many other

CENTRAL AMERICA AT A GLANCE

● Population density:
Belize, 10 people per square kilometre;
Costa Rica 69 people per square kilometre;
El Salvador, 287 people per square kilometre;
Guatemala, 104 people per square kilometre;
Honduras, 56 people per square kilometre;
Nicaragua, 39 people per square kilometre;
Panama, 37 people per square kilometre
● Largest cities (1992–95): Guatemala City
(Guatemala) 1,814,000; San Salvador
(El Salvador) 1,522,000; San José (Costa Rica)
1,186,000; Managua (Nicaragua) 973,000;
Tegucigalpa (Honduras) 739,000;
Panama City (Panama) 452,000
● Highest mountain: Volcano Tajumulca
(Guatemala), at 4,211 metres
● Largest body of water: Lake Nicaragua,
160 kilometres long with an area of 8,030
square kilometres
● Major religions: Roman Catholicism and
traditional beliefs
● Major resources: Agricultural produce,
shellfish, timber, iron, silver, copper, lead, tin,
HYDRO-ELECTRICITY and GEOTHERMAL ENERGY
● Major products: Bananas, coffee, fruit,
cotton, textiles, timber and minerals
● Environmental problems: SOIL EROSION,
DEFORESTATION, water and atmospheric pollution

▲ A stone mask of the sun at Copán in Honduras. These are the largest Mayan ruins in Central America. The city once covered an area of 39 square kilometres and is famous for its three-dimensional stone carvings.

◄ An aerial view of Panama City, one of the wealthiest areas in the whole of Central America.

INDIGENOUS peoples living in the region including the Lenca, Cuna and Miskito.

In the 16th century, Europeans arrived in Central America, attracted by rumours of gold and other riches. Their superior weapons enabled them to conquer the indigenous peoples. As a result, the region fell almost entirely under the control of the Spanish for 300 years. During the 19th century, however, the countries of the region gained their independence.

Central America is a region of great contrasts and you can find out more about the different countries of the area in this book.

THE LANDSCAPE

As they are situated on the narrow ISTHMUS between the land masses of North and South America, the countries of Central America are particularly vulnerable to earthquakes and volcanic eruptions. The region displays a remarkable variety of landscapes. These include active volcanoes rising to over 4,000 metres, tropical beaches, rainforests rich in wildlife and cool TEMPERATE highlands.

Central America extends for a distance of 1,900 kilometres from the Mexican border to Colombia, but it is only one quarter of the size of Mexico. It is bordered on the west by the Pacific Ocean and on the east by the Caribbean Sea and lies between the Equator and the Tropic of Cancer.

A chain of volcanoes that runs close to the Pacific Ocean dominates the landscape. Inland, lies a rugged upland landscape formed by ancient volcanic eruptions. This volcanic upland and the narrow Pacific coast is now home to nearly three-quarters of the population.

The eastern coastal landscape was formed by a different geological process, during which the earth's crust was compressed into a series of parallel ridges and valleys. This landscape extends across north-western Central America to the Caribbean coastline of Honduras. The ridges continue under the Caribbean Sea where the highest peaks re-emerge as the islands of the Greater Antilles.

One-third of the land in Central America lies above 1,000 metres. There are only small areas of low-lying land and these are restricted to the northern part of Guatemala,

▼ *The landscape of Central America is dominated by the cones of volcanoes like Poás, in Costa Rica.*

► *The typical landscape in the cool highlands of Guatemala consists of a patchwork of small fields on steep hillsides.*

◀ Ambergris Caye is just one of several hundred small coral islands off the coast of Belize.

the narrow coastal strips along the Pacific and Caribbean coastlines, and the lowlands that border Lakes Managua and Nicaragua in Nicaragua.

At the limits of the region, there are a number of interesting geographical features. In the extreme north, there is an area of undulating hills covered in rainforest, known as El Petén. This is the largest remaining area of rainforest in Central America. In the very south, is Darién, an area of Panama that consists of low, scrubby forest which is virtually uninhabited. Off the Caribbean coast of Belize, there are hundreds of small coral islands called cayes.

KEY FACTS

● The continents of North and South America were separated by a narrow strip of water until the end of the last Ice Age, 3 million years ago.
● Belize has the world's fifth longest barrier reef.
● More than 35,000 people have been killed by earthquakes in Guatemala and Nicaragua since 1970.
● The narrowest part of Central America is in Panama where only 80 kilometres of the Panama Canal separate the Atlantic from the Pacific Ocean.
● The region has more than 100 volcanoes, a number of which are still active.

CLIMATE AND WEATHER

◀ *The high levels of rainfall in the Sierra Mountains near Quiche in Guatemala enable the cool* MONTANE *rainforest to thrive.*

The whole of Central America is located in the tropics, but it is the altitude and the season rather than the latitude that determines the local conditions. As more than one-third of the land in the region is above 1,000 metres, the temperatures here are considerably cooler than the lowlands and the climate is temperate. The climate of the lowlands and the coasts is tropical.

Central America lies in the NORTHERN HEMISPHERE and, like Europe and North America, the hottest months are from April until September. At this time temperatures can soar to well above 30°C along the Caribbean coasts of countries like Belize, Honduras and Nicaragua. The coolest months are October to March. During these months temperatures can fall to only a few degrees above freezing in the highlands.

Four of the seven capitals are situated in the temperate highlands, where nearly two-thirds of the population of Central America live. Because of the seasonal rainfall and the fact that temperatures rarely fall to below 5°C, the highlands are ideal for many types of agriculture.

The heaviest rains, for the most part,

occur between April and September. Generally they begin in the south of the region and move north. For example, in April, Darién, in the South of Panama, can experience heavy rain, while Guatemala can still be waiting for its first rains at the end of May.

There is a distinct difference in rainfall between the Pacific and Caribbean coasts. The Pacific rains fall mainly between the months of April and September and the all-day rainstorms, called the temporales, occur in the months of June and September. In contrast, the Caribbean coast experiences heavy rainfall throughout the year. Between November and January, both the Pacific and Caribbean coasts are at risk from the devastating effects of hurricanes. From time to time, the weather of the whole of Central America can be affected by the EL NIÑO current in the Pacific Ocean.

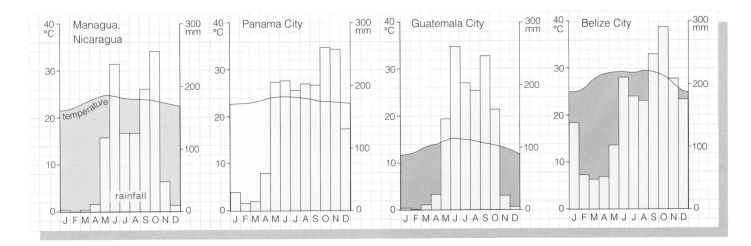

◀ **The coastal strip of El Salvador has a tropical climate and seasonal rains. These support the cultivation of crops such as coconuts, cotton and citrus fruit.**

KEY FACTS

● The annual rainfall along the Caribbean coast ranges from 3,500 mm to 7,000 mm each year.
● In 1988, Hurricane Joan devastated the banana harvest in Nicaragua and damaged the new fishing fleet and shrimp farms along the Caribbean coast.
● In 1998 the warm El Niño current disrupted the seasonal rains, causing widespread drought which led to poor harvests and bushfires.

A CHICLERO climbs a tree in the rainforest in El Petén, Guatemala, to cut channels in the bark so that the chicle sap can be collected.

AGRICULTURE

Central America is an area rich in natural resources. The most important of these is its fertile volcanic soils that are ideally suited to agriculture. It was the excellent conditions for growing food that enabled large civilizations like the Mayas to flourish many centuries before the arrival of Europeans. The Mayas and other Indians grew maize and beans as their staple crops and millions of people still rely on these foodstuffs.

Today, the region's main natural resource is still its agricultural land. Agriculture accounts for between half and three-quarters of the total value of exports from each country. The main products are maize, coffee, sorghum, bananas and sugar.

In some countries, such as El Salvador, nearly all land suitable for agriculture has been converted into farmland. Other countries, such as Honduras and Belize, have the opportunity to expand the amount of land used for agriculture.

FORESTRY

In several of the countries, such as Guatemala, Honduras, Panama and Belize, there are large expanses of tropical forests. Honduras has 4.1 million hectares of forest cover and a further 2.5 million suitable for re-afforestation. However, forestry resources are disappearing rapidly. In the El Petén region of Guatemala, half the tropical forest has already been cut down. The wood of the mahogany tree is very valuable and it is harvested in Panama, Belize and Guatemala. Chicle, an ingredient of chewing gum, is tapped from rainforest trees in Belize and Guatemala.

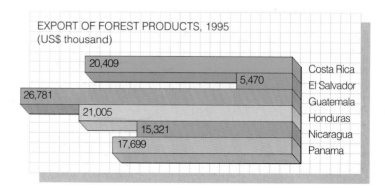

EXPORT OF FOREST PRODUCTS, 1995 (US$ thousand)

Costa Rica	20,409
El Salvador	5,470
Guatemala	26,781
Honduras	21,005
Nicaragua	15,321
Panama	17,699

MINERALS

Most countries in the region have only modest mineral reserves, with the exception of Honduras and Nicaragua. Honduras has considerable reserves of silver, gold, lead, zinc, iron, copper and antimony, but only silver, lead, zinc and small amounts of gold are mined commercially. Nicaragua has unexploited deposits of copper, lead, zinc, cadmium, bismuth, platinum, iron, magnesium, chrome and titanium. Mining in Nicaragua, especially of gold, is likely to increase. Nicaragua also has the largest deposits of calcium carbonate (used in the manufacture of cement) in the region.

Among those countries with small mineral reserves, El Salvador has small deposits of gold, silver, mercury, lead, zinc, salt and limestone. Costa Rica has deposits of manganese, mercury and gold and is an exporter of sulphur and iron ore. Panama's main mineral resource is copper and Guatemala's is nickel.

▼ *Countries such as Belize, Guatemala and Honduras are cutting down large numbers of rainforest trees for timber to export to Europe, USA and Japan.*

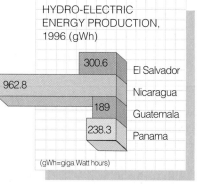

HYDRO-ELECTRIC ENERGY PRODUCTION, 1996 (gWh)

300.6 El Salvador

962.8 Nicaragua

189 Guatemala

238.3 Panama

(gWh=giga Watt hours)

▲ **Heat from deep in the earth is used to create the steam to power the turbines that produce electricity at this geothermal power plant.**

FOSSIL FUELS

All seven countries consume large quantities of oil and other fossil fuels which, until recently, have been almost entirely imported. Exploration is underway in a number of countries and significant oil deposits have been located in El Salvador and Guatemala. Guatemala produced

KEY FACTS

● Deposits of iron ore in Costa Rica are estimated to be 400 million tonnes. Deposits of sulphur are estimated to be 11 million tonnes.

● The geothermal power plant at Ahuachapan in El Salvador produces 60 megawatts of electricity, which is 10% of the total electricity consumed in the country.

● Honduras harvested 3.8 million cubic metres of timber in 1994.

● Maize, avocados and chocolate all originated in Central America.

● Forest and woodland account for 54% of the total area of Panama.

5,330,000 barrels of oil in 1996, 87% of which was exported. Honduras is the only country with large coal deposits.

ELECTRICITY

Central America has both heavy rainfall and a mountainous terrain, and these are the key requirements for the working of hydro-electric power plants. These make a major contribution to the region's energy needs. For example, 80% of Honduras' electricity needs are met by hydro-electric power stations. A massive 3.34 million kilowatt hours of electricity was produced in 1996 in El Salvador and half of this came from just four hydro-electric power stations. Countries in the region can also tap into the geothermal energy of the land in order to produce electricity.

TOURISM

The magnificent landscape of towering volcanoes, dense rainforests and tropical beaches are an important attraction for tourists. As the political troubles that have plagued Central America in recent years have died down, there have been increasing numbers of tourists visiting the region. Guatemala alone had more than half a million tourist visitors in 1996.

▼ *Avocados occur naturally in Central America and are cultivated in many areas like this one, near Lake Atitlán, in Guatemala.*

THE ORIGINS OF THE POPULATION

The ancestors of Central America's indigenous people are believed to have crossed the Bering Straits – between what is now Siberia and Alaska – and travelled south, to reach Central America sometime between 10,000 and 20,000 years ago. By the time the first Europeans arrived, the Central American Indian population, which was made up of many distinct cultures, was estimated to be around 5 million.

The arrival of the Spanish in the 16th

▼ *A farmer with oxen in Costa Rica. Here, most landowners and farmers tend to come from a predominantly white background.*

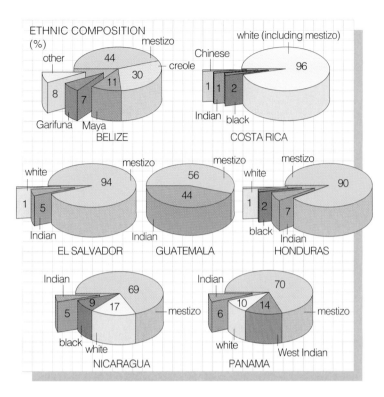

ETHNIC COMPOSITION (%)

BELIZE: other 8, Garifuna 7, Maya 11, creole 30, mestizo 44

COSTA RICA: Indian 1, black 1, Chinese 2, white (including mestizo) 96

EL SALVADOR: Indian 1, white 5, mestizo 94

GUATEMALA: Indian 44, mestizo 56

HONDURAS: Indian 1, black 2, white 7, mestizo 90

NICARAGUA: black 5, white 9, Indian 17, mestizo 69

PANAMA: white 6, Indian 10, West Indian 14, mestizo 70

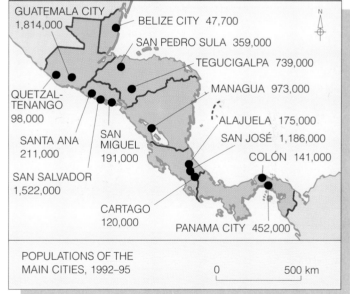

One-third of the population of Costa Rica live in the bustling, cosmopolitan city of San José.

POPULATION LIVING IN URBAN AREAS, 1993
(% of total population)

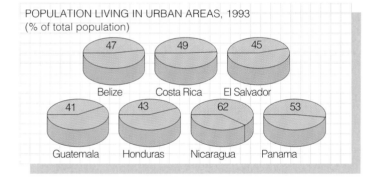

47	49	45
Belize	Costa Rica	El Salvador
41	43	62	53
Guatemala	Honduras	Nicaragua	Panama

GUATEMALA CITY 1,814,000
BELIZE CITY 47,700
SAN PEDRO SULA 359,000
TEGUCIGALPA 739,000
MANAGUA 973,000
QUETZAL-TENANGO 98,000
ALAJUELA 175,000
SAN JOSÉ 1,186,000
SANTA ANA 211,000
SAN MIGUEL 191,000
COLÓN 141,000
SAN SALVADOR 1,522,000
CARTAGO 120,000
PANAMA CITY 452,000

POPULATIONS OF THE MAIN CITIES, 1992–95

0   500 km

century had a dramatic effect on these indigenous populations. The settlers brought diseases like smallpox with them, to which the local people had little resistance. The Spanish ruthlessly exploited the indigenous people, forcing many of them to work as labourers in mines and plantations. Millions of Indians died during the first century of contact with the Spanish.

During the colonial period, which lasted around 300 years, the European settlers established major cities such as Tegucigalpa, Antigua, Managua and San Salvador. Many European men married indigenous women and their descendants are known as mestizos.

Some sections of the population are descended from the black slaves who were brought to work on coffee and sugar plantations. From around 1850, many black slaves were moved to Central America

● After the arrival of Europeans in the 16th century, the population of Central America crashed and it was not until 1930 that it recovered to its pre-16th century level of 5 million.

● Honduras has the highest population growth rate in the region and its population is projected to be over 9 million in the year 2020.

● Belize is the smallest Central American country, with a population of 228,000.

● The average population density per square kilometre for Central America is 67. This figure is 243 for the UK and 28 for the USA.

● The percentage of people living in urban areas in Honduras rose from 29% in 1970 to 48% in 1995 and that in Nicaragua from 47% to 63%.

● In Nicaragua, 9 out of 10 people live in the area between the Pacific and the western shores of Lake Nicaragua.

● Costa Rica has more than 35,000 settlers from North America living in the country.

● Belmopan replaced Belize City as the capital of Belize in 1970 after the former capital was severely damaged by a hurricane in 1961. In 1993, it had a population of 3,800.

▼ *The Indians of the Guatemalan highlands wear colourful shawls, called huípiles, that are distinctive within each village.*

from the islands in the Caribbean to help build the railways and the Panama Canal. People of mixed black and Indian race are called mulattos.

THE POPULATION TODAY

Because of the history of the region, the population of Central America is very varied. Mestizos (sometimes also called Latinos) make up around half of the entire population, although they now account for as much as 94% of the population in

El Salvador. There are also distinct indigenous groups, such as the Misquito of Honduras and Nicaragua, the Cuna of Panama, and the descendants of the Maya in Guatemala.

Throughout the region, Indians account for one-fifth of the population. Their numbers vary widely between the seven countries as does their position in society. Most are concentrated in Guatemala, where between 60 and 70% of the population are AMERINDIANS of Maya origin

and speak one of the 22 distinct Mayan languages as their first language.

In Panama, there are five different indigenous peoples. These include the Gyami Indians of West Panama, who are the most numerous, with 123,000 tribal members. In Panama, the Indians play an active role in government. The Cuna Indians, for example, have their own tribal land where they keep alive many of their traditions. They also have their own political representatives in Panama's Legislative Assembly. In Costa Rica, however, only 1% of the population belong to an indigenous group and whites are, therefore, dominant. Blacks and mulattos

▶ *A Cuna Indian woman selling local handicrafts on San Blas island, Panama.*

are the most numerous in Panama and the Caribbean coastal plain. In Belize, Honduras and Guatemala, a distinct ethnic group called the Garifuna are to be found. They are descended from Carib Indians and black slaves and live in fishing villages along the coast.

MIGRATION

Before the arrival of the Spanish in the 16th century, the Indian peoples often migrated throughout the region. The Cuna of Panama, for example, originally came from Colombia. During the 20th century, however, the populations of all seven countries have tended to migrate from the countryside to the towns. Many rural areas of Central America lack the most basic services of schools and hospitals. In addition, the best employment opportunities are to be found in the main economic centres. This has led people to move to the capitals or other major cities, in search of a better life.

In the second half of this century, fierce fighting occurred in most of the countries of Central America and this had the effect of speeding up the movement of people from the countryside to the towns. It also led to thousands of people becoming refugees in other countries. In 1992, 114,000 refugees from other parts of the region were living in Costa Rica.

POPULATION GROWTH

During the 20th century, the populations of all seven countries have grown. The growth rate is now slowing in the wealthier countries such as Costa Rica (2.2%) and Panama (1.7%). However, the population of Honduras is growing at 3% per year. The percentage of the population under the age of fifteen is much higher than countries such as Germany (16%), Japan (18%) or Canada (21%). People below the age of fifteen account for 44% of the population of Nicaragua and 33% of the population of Panama.

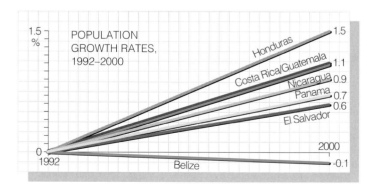

POPULATION GROWTH RATES, 1992–2000

Honduras — 1.5
Costa Rica/Guatemala — 1.1
Nicaragua — 0.9
Panama — 0.7
— 0.6
El Salvador

1.5 %

0

1992

2000

Belize — -0.1

DAILY LIFE

FAMILY LIFE

Generally speaking, within Central America, families are still large and play an important part in everyday life. It is, therefore, common for parents, children, cousins and grandparents to live close to one another. However, this situation is changing as more people leave the area in which they grew up and head to the large cities in order to find work.

In the cities, some families live in luxury while others live in dreadful poverty. Home, for many people, is a modern apartment and many are employed in professional occupations such as banking, computer programming and law. A small proportion of these people are extremely rich and can afford private planes and luxury yachts. This is in contrast to the millions of people who live in extreme poverty in the shanty towns that surround most of the main cities.

The bulk of the rural population, however, is made up of farmers and their families, who produce just enough food to feed themselves. Here the family is very important, and often children and relatives

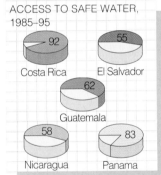

ACCESS TO SAFE WATER, 1985–95

92 Costa Rica
55 El Salvador
62 Guatemala
58 Nicaragua
83 Panama

◀ *Many wealthy families in Costa Rica have a luxury house in the capital and a cattle ranch in the countryside.*

23

all work together on the land. The family is also central to the culture of the indigenous people in the region, such as the Cuna and Quiche Maya. They maintain their traditional communities and people of all ages play an active part in daily life.

RELIGION

The main religion of six of the seven countries in Central America is Roman Catholicism. Belize, until recently, has been predominantly Protestant, but the Spanish-speaking sector of the population is growing rapidly and so is the number of Catholics.

Roman Catholics account for 85% of the population of Panama, and 95% of the population of Costa Rica. The black populations along the Caribbean coast tend to be Protestants.

▶ *Easter and Holy Week are among the most important religious festivals in the region. Here a young boy in traditional purple robes is dispensing incense at the Easter celebration.*

MAJOR FESTIVALS AND HOLIDAYS

BELIZE

March/April	EASTER
21 April	QUEEN'S BIRTHDAY
1 May	LABOUR DAY
10 September	ST GEORGE'S CAYE DAY
	This was where a battle was fought in 1798 that gave Britain possession of the territory
21 September	INDEPENDENCE DAY
19 November	GARIFUNA SETTLEMENT DAY
	This re-enacts the time in 1823 when the Garifuna were forced to flee after a failed rebellion in Honduras

COSTA RICA

19 March	SAINT JOSEPH'S DAY
11 April	BATTLE OF RIVAS
	This was when Costa Rica's national hero, Juan Santamaría, sacrificed his life fighting against a private army of invaders from the USA.
March/April	EASTER
1 May	LABOUR DAY
25 July	GUANACASTE DAY
	The state of Guanacaste remained independent until 1824 when it opted to join the rest of Costa Rica
15 September	INDEPENDENCE DAY
1 November	ALL SAINTS' DAY

GUATEMALA

March/April	EASTER
1 May	LABOUR DAY
15 September	INDEPENDENCE DAY
20 October	REVOLUTION DAY
1 November	ALL SAINTS' DAY

NICARAGUA

March/April	EASTER
1 May	LABOUR DAY
19 July	REVOLUTION 1979 DAY
14 September	BATTLE OF SAN JACINTO
15 September	INDEPENDENCE DAY
1 November	ALL SAINTS' DAY

▶ *There are many religious days and festivals in Central America. One of these is the annual festival of Sololá, a small town in the hills above Lake Atitlán, in Guatemala. This takes place every August.*

EDUCATION

Education for children between 6 and 14 is compulsory in all seven countries but, in spite of this, school attendance is generally poor. In rural areas many children do not complete their education because they are needed to work either on the family farm or in low-paid employment such as coffee harvesting to help support their families. People who live in urban areas and who can pay for private schools have the best educational opportunities.

Literacy levels have risen throughout the region over the last 20 years. For example, the percentage of adults who can read and write in Panama has improved from 81% to 90% between 1972 and 1990. However,

PUPILS PER PRIMARY TEACHER, 1995

25	Belize
32	Costa Rica
44	El Salvador
34	Guatemala
38	Honduras
37	Nicaragua

◀ *Many rural schools in Central America have only the most basic equipment for the classrooms.*

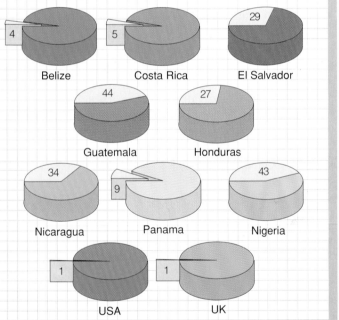

POPULATION UNABLE TO READ OR WRITE, 1995
(% of total population)

Belize 4
Costa Rica 5
El Salvador 29
Guatemala 44
Honduras 27
Nicaragua 34
Panama 9
Nigeria 43
USA 1
UK 1

literacy levels are still poor when compared to most other countries in the northern hemisphere.

SOCIAL PROBLEMS

The region has a number of major social problems including poverty, poor health facilities, violent crime and drug trafficking. Honduras, for example, is the poorest country in the northern hemisphere. Here, people had a life expectancy of only 68 in 1996. It also has the highest levels of diseases like malaria, AIDS and tuberculosis of any Central American country. The rural populations of all the countries suffer from poor diets and limited health care facilities.

Most of the Central American countries have recently suffered war, civil war and high levels of violent crime. Although the 1990s have seen an improvement in human rights, countries like El Salvador are still violent places. In Guatemala, the violence and appalling poverty experienced over the last two decades by the poorest people has led to a huge increase in the numbers of homeless children who live on the streets.

Central America is a major route for the trafficking of drugs from South America to

North America. The demand for illegal drugs in North America has stimulated this multi-million dollar trade. In recent years, for example, many Belizeans have become involved in the production of cannabis. The export of cannabis from Belize is now estimated to be worth about US$ 100 million a year.

1,136	Costa Rica
1,563	El Salvador
2,000	Guatemala
1,266	Honduras
2,000	Nicaragua
562	Panama
300	UK
420	USA

POPULATION PER DOCTOR, 1985–95

LEISURE

As in most Roman Catholic countries, occasions such as christenings and first communion are considered important and are celebrated by all the family. There are many religious festivals, the most important of which are Christmas, Holy Week and the Day of the Dead on 2 November.

The most popular sport in Central America is football. Volleyball is also a major sport and this, along with football, is taught in schools. These are not the only sports. Belizeans enjoy cricket and, in rural areas, cock-fighting and bull-fighting are still popular pastimes.

Music is an important part of life in all seven countries. The music in the north of the region is influenced by Mexico, but Guatemala has its own musical style based around a large wooden xylophone, called a marimba. Panama has a distinct musical tradition which is based on a combination of African and Colombian influences. Many indigenous peoples such as the Chorotegas of Costa Rica have kept their traditional musical heritage.

▶ *Costa Rica narrowly missed a place in the 1998 World Cup finals when they lost to Jamaica.*

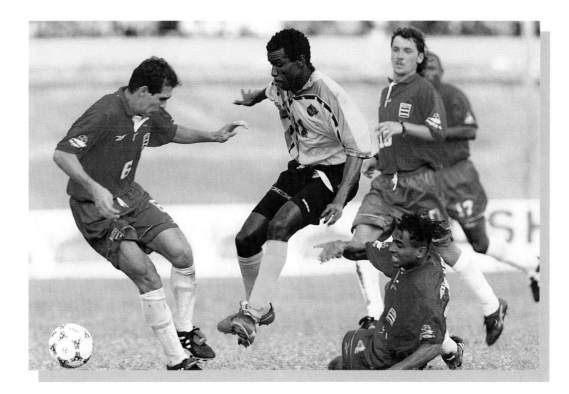

RULE AND LAW

The political history of most of the Spanish-speaking countries within Central America has been a turbulent one since they gained independence from Spain during the 19th century. In recent years, the region has seen wars, civil uprisings, dictatorships and terrorism. An exception to this is Costa Rica where, after a revolution in 1948, a democratic constitution was put in place and the army replaced by a civil guard.

The recent political instability in Nicaragua is, however, typical of the region. Here, in July 1979, a popular uprising overthrew the corrupt government of President Garcia Somoza. This ended 20 years of dictatorship, which had cost the lives of over 50,000 Nicaraguans. The opposition to the Somoza family was led by a political group called the Sandinistas who were supported by the Soviet Union. They went on to win elections in 1985. The USA, however, provided military training and weapons for the CONTRAS, who opposed the newly elected government. The USA feared the expansion of Soviet influence in Central America. They also imposed a trade ban on Nicaragua. The conflict was finally resolved by negotiation

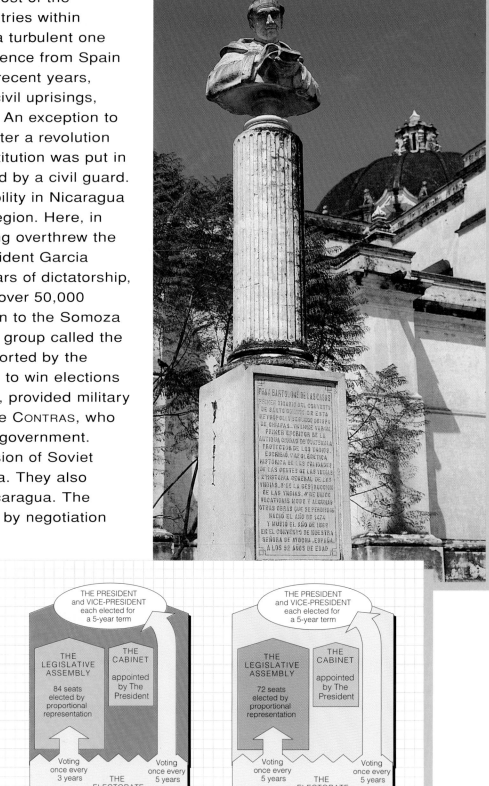

BELIZE

THE QUEEN OF ENGLAND

appoints

GOVERNOR GENERAL — *appoints* → THE PRIME MINISTER

THE NATIONAL ASSEMBLY

28 seats elected by proportional representation

THE SENATE
8 members

5 appointed by Prime Minister

2 appointed by the leader of the opposition

1 appointed by the Governor General

THE ELECTORATE
Voting once every 5 years

EL SALVADOR

THE PRESIDENT and VICE-PRESIDENT each elected for a 5-year term

THE LEGISLATIVE ASSEMBLY

84 seats elected by proportional representation

THE CABINET

appointed by The President

Voting once every 3 years

Voting once every 5 years

THE ELECTORATE

PANAMA

THE PRESIDENT and VICE-PRESIDENT each elected for a 5-year term

THE LEGISLATIVE ASSEMBLY

72 seats elected by proportional representation

THE CABINET

appointed by The President

Voting once every 5 years

Voting once every 5 years

THE ELECTORATE

◀ *A statue of Bartolomé de las Casas, who championed the rights of the indigenous people of Guatemala in 1533.*

in 1987, with the two sides attempting to work together. In 1990, a new president was elected but the unrest has continued.

Some of the countries in Central America have the worst human rights records of any region in the world. In Guatemala, during the 1980s, an army officer called Rios Montt organized a campaign to crush guerrillas in the Guatemalan highlands. They were fighting for fair access to land

KEY FACTS

● In 1980, a civil war broke out in El Salvador. When peace terms were agreed in 1991, about 75,000 people had been killed, hundreds of thousands had been made homeless and more than 50% of the workforce were unemployed.

● In 1989, US troops invaded Panama to remove President Manuel Noriega, who was involved in organized drug trafficking. He was tried in the USA and found guilty in 1992.

● In 1992, Rigoberta Menchu, a Mayan Indian, won the Nobel Peace prize for her work in seeking peace between the Mayan people and the military government of Guatemala.

and representation in government. In the first year alone, 15,000 Guatemalans were killed, hundreds of villages burnt and 70,000 people were forced to take refuge in Mexico. Civil government was restored in 1986, but the military continued to abuse human rights. The situation has improved since 1996, when the government and the left-wing rebels signed a detailed peace agreement.

During the 1990s, the countries of Central America have grown relatively more peaceful and all now have democratic governments with an elected assembly.

◀ *Sandino Day in Managua on which the life of Augusto Cesar Sandino is celebrated. He organized a rebellion against the US occupation of Nicaragua in 1927. He was killed by national guardsmen in 1934.*

FOOD AND FARMING

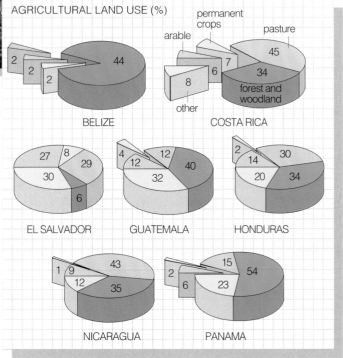

AGRICULTURAL LAND USE (%)

BELIZE
2 2 2 44

COSTA RICA
permanent crops
arable
pasture 45
7
34
forest and woodland
8
6
other

EL SALVADOR
27 8
30 29
6

GUATEMALA
4 12
12 40
32

HONDURAS
2 30
14
20 34

NICARAGUA
1 9 43
12 35

PANAMA
15 54
2
6 23

Agriculture forms the mainstay of the economies of all seven countries. For example, in Honduras, agriculture employs 38% of the work force and accounted for 21% of the GROSS DOMESTIC PRODUCT (GDP) in 1995. In Guatemala, about 50% of the work force are employed in agriculture. In El Salvador, agriculture employed 25% of the work force in 1996 and accounted for 33% of exports and 70% of domestic food requirements.

At present, however, agriculture is declining in importance in relation to other sectors of the economy. For example, in Costa Rica, 47% of the labour force was involved in agriculture in 1965 compared with 20.3% in 1995. Sugar, coffee and bananas continue to be the most important crops in the region, but cattle rearing is in decline. Fishing and fish-farming, however, are becoming increasingly important.

In addition to commercial agriculture, millions of people in Central America are involved in subsistence farming, often on just a few hectares of land. This means they can only produce enough food to provide for the requirements of the household or village. Poor farmers make up nearly three-quarters of all rural inhabitants in the region. Typically they produce maize, beans and squash which make up a large part of their diet. Throughout much of Central America, subsistence agriculture still follows the MILPA tradition. This involves the interplanting or mixing of crops in the same plot and is a similar system to that used by the Mayas.

Depending on the climate, some of these farmers may also produce grain, fruit, vegetables and meat products for the commercial market. They also provide the cheap seasonal labour required for the coffee, banana and sugar harvests.

CASH CROPS

In general, coffee is the main crop in the volcanic uplands. The other four of the five main exports, sugar, bananas, cattle and cotton, are grown in the lowland plains.

Coffee is the most important agricultural export for El Salvador, Guatemala, Honduras and Nicaragua. In Belize, sugar and citrus fruits account for 40% of total agricultural production and 80% of exports. Bananas are the single most important agricultural product in both Costa Rica and Panama. Other crops that are grown on a large scale for export include cotton, cut flowers, tobacco, ornamental plants and spices such as cardamom.

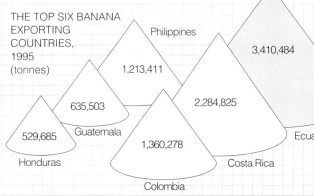

THE TOP SIX BANANA EXPORTING COUNTRIES, 1995 (tonnes)

Philippines 1,213,411

3,410,484

635,503

2,284,825

Guatemala

529,685

Honduras

1,360,278

Ecuador

Costa Rica

Colombia

▶ *Thousands of people are employed in the harvesting and processing of bananas, such as these Guaymi Indians in a packing plant in Panama.*

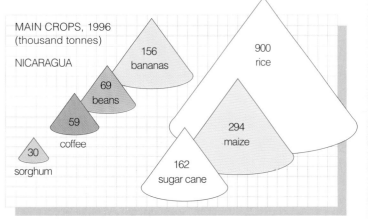

This dish is typical of the food served in Nicaragua. It includes chicken, TORTILLAS, salad and gallo pinto, which consists of rice and beans.

MAIN CROPS, 1996
(thousand tonnes)

NICARAGUA

156 bananas
900 rice
69 beans
59 coffee
294 maize
30 sorghum
162 sugar cane

FISH

Shell fish are rapidly becoming one of the region's biggest exports. In Panama, shell fish have already become the country's second most valuable export, earning US$ 87.2 million in 1995. Similarly, Honduras earned US$ 178.2 million from shrimp and lobster exports in 1996, and the export of shell fish from Nicaragua rose to US$ 74.6

million in 1995. Three-quarters of Nicaragua's fish and shellfish production is exported to the USA.

All the countries in the region have realized that fishing could be a major contributor to their economies in the future, and many are investing in expanding their fishing fleets. Costa Rica already has a major fishing fleet and earned US$ 87.2 million from its catches of tuna, sardine, shrimp and shark. However, if more and more fish are caught each year, overfishing could lead to a serious reduction of fish stocks in the future.

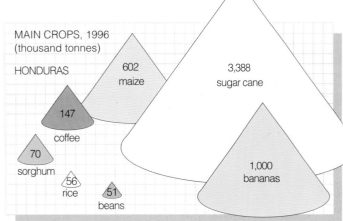

MAIN CROPS, 1996
(thousand tonnes)

HONDURAS

602 maize
3,388 sugar cane
147 coffee
70 sorghum
56 rice
51 beans
1,000 bananas

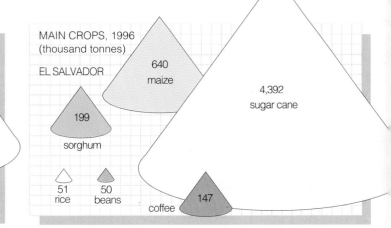

MAIN CROPS, 1996
(thousand tonnes)

EL SALVADOR

640 maize
4,392 sugar cane
199 sorghum
51 rice
50 beans
147 coffee

KEY FACTS

- Panama's chicken-meat industry has grown rapidly and now there are more than 9 million chickens on farms throughout the country.
- The average size of a coffee plantation in Costa Rica is only 10 hectares, but most plantations are technically advanced and among the most efficient in the world.
- Agricultural products such as coffee, sugar and bananas account for 75% of El Salvador's export earnings.
- Bananas accounted for 36% of total agricultural revenue in Panama in 1996.
- Honduras has a total land area of 11.2 million hectares yet only 1.8 million hectares is used for arable crops and permanent crops.
- Guatemala is the world's largest producer of cardamoms exporting 13,000 tonnes in 1994.
- Nicaragua earned US$ 671 million from agriculture in 1996.

LIVESTOCK

During the 1970s and 1980s, tens of thousands of hectares of forest were cleared to create pasture for cattle ranching. During this era, the ranches provided cut-price beef for the large hamburger chains in the USA. Livestock rearing remains an important part of the economy in Panama and Costa Rica. However, in the last decade, cattle ranching generally has declined in importance and, for example, only accounted for 7.5% of GDP in Nicaragua in 1995.

 *The market in the Guatemalan town of Chichicastenango displays produce that is typical of the cool highlands of Guatemala.*

TRADE AND INDUSTRY

Industrialization only began in the region in the 1950s. Up until then, the economies of each country had been almost entirely based on agriculture. Today, most of the manufacturing economies are still dominated by food processing and beverage companies.

During the 1970s and 1980s, new industries, such as the manufacture of pharmaceuticals or the production of paper were developed. Maquilladora industries were also created. In these, brand-named products, usually well known in Japan or the USA, are made under licence, at a much lower cost than is possible in either of those two countries. The economies of some Central American countries also have important service sectors, especially where American banking or computer centres are based.

The main trading partner of Central American countries has been the USA, but there is a considerable amount of trade within Central America and also with Europe.

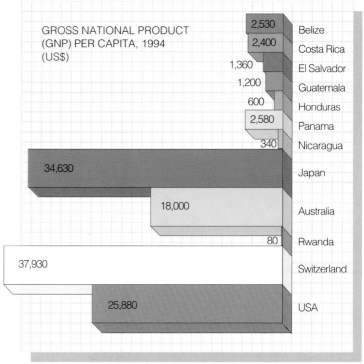

GROSS NATIONAL PRODUCT (GNP) PER CAPITA, 1994 (US$)

Belize	2,530
Costa Rica	2,400
El Salvador	1,360
Guatemala	1,200
Honduras	600
Panama	2,580
Nicaragua	340
Japan	34,630
Australia	18,000
Rwanda	80
Switzerland	37,930
USA	25,880

▼ *There are many small businesses in Nicaragua. This man is making furniture out of local wood.*

COSTA RICA

Costa Rica has a well-developed economy and is the most industrialized country in the region. Manufacturing and mining account for 20% of GDP. However, in 1995, tourism became the single largest earner of foreign currency. The country's most important industry is food processing, and its main trading partner is the USA. Costa Rica also has a booming service sector including banking and computer operating centres.

EL SALVADOR

El Salvador's economy is still dependent on agriculture and, today, new crops such as cut flowers, soya beans and ornamental plants are also being grown. The most important manufacturing industries are food processing and petroleum products. Other key industries include textiles, pharmaceuticals, shoes, fertilizers, cosmetics, cement and rubber goods. Maquilladora industries employ over 20,000 people and produce garments such as jeans.

▲ *Much of the agricultural work carried out in the coastal plain of El Salvador is highly mechanized, like on this pineapple plantation.*

BELIZE

Belize has the second highest per capita income in the region but its economy is quite different from that of Panama. Belize relies on a limited number of agricultural products and tourism as the mainstays of its economy. For example, agriculture accounts for 40% of the nation's GDP and 75% of its exports. Sugar and citrus fruits are its main exports and the USA is its main trading partner. Tourism earns more than $100 million a year in foreign exchange.

KEY FACTS

● Tourism has become Costa Rica's main foreign currency earner. In 1995, Costa Rica earned US$ 661 million dollars from tourism, compared to US$ 620 million for bananas and US$ 407 million from coffee.

● Nicaragua earned US$ 21 million from tourism in 1992. In 1996, the figure had risen to US$ 58.2 million.

● When newcomers are granted Belizean nationality, Belize earns £75,000 per family. Belize limits the number of incomers to 500 a year.

● Agricultural products such as coffee, sugar and bananas account for 75% of El Salvador's export earnings.

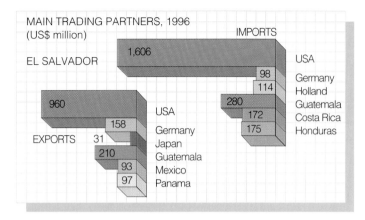

MAIN TRADING PARTNERS, 1996
(US$ million)

IMPORTS

EL SALVADOR 1,606

USA
98
Germany
114
Holland
280
Guatemala
172
Costa Rica
175
Honduras

960

USA

158

EXPORTS 31

Germany
Japan
210
Guatemala
93
Mexico
97
Panama

GUATEMALA

Although half the workforce of Guatemala are employed in agriculture, there are many manufacturing industries, like food and beverage production, in urban locations. Other industries include the manufacture of vehicle tyres, the refining of petroleum products and a large clothing industry. Many products are brand-named maquilladora goods destined for the USA. The tourism industry is very important to Guatemala. It was badly affected by the conflicts between the army and terrorists in the 1980s, but is now beginning to recover.

▲ *The streets in Guatemala City are often very busy as people shop for cut-price items like locally made jeans or televisions.*

NICARAGUA

Nicaragua's economy was devastated in the 1980s by the Sandinista–Contra conflict and a subsequent trade embargo imposed by the USA. Agriculture is still the main sector of the economy, earning US $671 million in 1996, but the manufacturing sector is developing rapidly. Industries include food processing, chemical plants, metal products, textiles, clothing, petroleum refining, beverages and footwear. In 1996, Nicaragua exported computer equipment worth US$ 112 million.

HONDURAS

Honduras is one of the poorest countries in the western hemisphere and remains far less industrialized than its neighbours. However, foreign investment has been helping to expand the food processing sector and to set up industries such as textiles, paper-making, soft drinks, cement, beer, cooking oil and rum. The country has the potential to expand its tourist and maquilladora industries, which have grown rapidly since 1982. However, bananas, coffee and shrimps continue to account for more than half of all exports.

PANAMA

Panama has the highest per capita income in the region and is set for major economic growth. It has an excellent strategic geographical position and a number of major economic assets. These include the Colon Duty Free Zone, an international banking

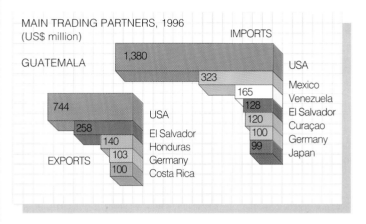

MAIN TRADING PARTNERS, 1996
(US$ million)

GUATEMALA

IMPORTS

1,380

EXPORTS

744
258
140
103
100

USA
El Salvador
Honduras
Germany
Costa Rica

323
165
128
120
100
99

USA

Mexico
Venezuela
El Salvador
Curaçao
Germany
Japan

sector, the Canal zone, the trans-isthmus oil pipeline and the Panama Canal. In addition, it has large agricultural, industrial and mining sectors.

Today, although bananas and shellfish are still the two largest exports, services such as banking and tourism are set to become increasingly important.

▲ *The capital cities like Guatemala City and Panama City have modern tower blocks housing international banks and a stock exchange.*

▶ *The magnificent Mayan ruins of Copán in Honduras attracts tens of thousands of visitors each year.*

TRANSPORT

The first modern means of transport in Central America were railways constructed in the 19th century to carry produce such as coffee and bananas to the ports for export. In the 1950s, as the economies of the countries of Central America began to grow, major improvements were made in the transport system.

Today, the railways have declined in importance and some countries, like Belize and Nicaragua, no longer have railways at all. Most countries, like Guatemala, have developed a comprehensive network of roads to connect all areas of the country.

The most important road is the Pan-American Highway which extends from Guatemala almost to the border with Colombia, connecting all the countries of Central America except Belize. A large number of the roads in Central America are unpaved. Costa Rica, for example, has an extensive network of 35,532 kilometres of roads, of which only 17% are paved.

Air travel has become increasingly important and each country has at least one international airport and a network of national air routes. Air travel has been expanded to cope with the increasing numbers of tourists and also the export of some of the non-traditional exports such as cut flowers and shellfish.

Along the Caribbean coast, travel by boat is often the only way to reach some areas, such as the swampy coasts of Honduras and Nicaragua. Also the bulk of exports and imports are handled by the modern

KEY FACTS

● The Pan-American Highway runs the length of Central America and ends at Yaviza in Panama. It is only possible to travel overland to South America on foot.

● Nicaragua sold the tracks of its disused railways for scrap metal.

● The Garifuna community of Stan Creek in Belize has a population of 10,000 people, but is only accessible by boat.

● In 1996, there were 333,990 cars in El Salvador.

● Air traffic in Costa Rica has more than doubled between 1986 and 1994.

●. At midday, on 31 December 1999, Panama will take over full control of the Panama Canal from the USA.

▲ **Guatemala City and many other large cities in Central America have serious traffic congestion and suffer problems with air pollution from vehicle exhausts.**

◀ **The Panama Canal was completed on 15 August 1914 and, since then, it has been used by more than 800,000 ships.**

LENGTH OF PAVED ROADS, 1992–93 (km)

Belize	Costa Rica	El Salvador	Guatemala
336	5,608	1,740	12,033

Honduras	Nicaragua	Panama	UK	USA
2,533	4,000	323	21,027	143,500

commercial ports on the Caribbean and Pacific coasts. Half of all Honduras's exports, for example, pass through Puerto Cortez, on the north coast.

The Panama Canal is one of the most important trade routes in the world. Today it takes a ship on average 24 hours to travel along the 80-kilometre canal and its locks. Before the canal was built, ships crossing from the Pacific to the Atlantic would have to round Cape Horn, at the southern tip of South America, adding several thousand kilometres to their journey.

Central America is facing many environmental challenges as its population grows and the economies in the region develop. The population is already over 35 million and has the second highest rate of growth in the world. To feed the many new mouths, more land will be needed to grow food, increasing the pressure to convert natural areas into farmland. Major environmental problems facing Central America are deforestation, air and water pollution, soil erosion, overfishing and a reduction in BIODIVERSITY.

Central America is particularly rich in wildlife, because the isthmus links the two distinct continents of North and South

▲ *The rapid growth of cities has led to many environmental problems in the slum areas. Here children play near an open sewer in Guatemala City.*

KEY FACTS

● El Petén, the largest continuous area of rainforest in Central America, accounts for 33% of the land area of Guatemala. The population of the area has risen rapidly from just 15,000 in 1950 to over 350,000 in 1997.
● Central America has more than 800 species of birds and is situated on three of the four major migration routes between North and South America.
● Panama alone has more bird species than the USA and Canada combined.
● One single tree on the island nature reserve of Barro Colorado was found to be home to 950 different species of beetle.
● Central America's natural forests are being cleared at the rate of 50 hectares per hour.
● The coral reefs off the coast of Belize are the fifth largest in the world and attract thousands of tourists every year.
● The region's population is predicted to rise from 35 million to 66 million by the year 2030.

America. As a consequence, Central America has a large number of different animal and plant species in relation to its size. For example, the region covers just 0.5% of the earth's surface yet it contains an estimated 8% of all the species on the planet. These species are found in a wide variety of habitats ranging from cloud forest to semi-desert.

Today, about one-third of the region's forest remains but deforestation continues at an alarming rate, calculated to be

400,000 hectares per year. Typically, loggers create routes into the forests and cut down valuable trees. Landless people then move in along the roads created by the loggers and clear the remaining forest to grow subsistence crops. The land becomes exhausted within three to four years and the farmers then move on, clearing new areas of forest.

Cattle ranching is the single largest cause of deforestation, accounting for the destruction of more than half of Central America's forests. In the 1960s and 1970s, large areas were cleared to provide pasture for the production of beef. After seven to ten years, the land became degraded and the ranchers had to keep moving on to find new pastures.

In response to the environmental catastrophe of deforestation, all the countries of Central America are making efforts to protect their remaining natural habitats. Today there are 18 million hectares of protected areas in the region and all countries have signed the Convention on Biological Diversity.

There are many problems facing the growing urban areas of Central America. Air pollution is a major problem in most of the large cities of the region. Costa Rica, for example, has over half a million vehicles, but there are few regulations on the exhaust gas emitted by each vehicle. The industrial areas also contribute to air pollution. Heavy industries such as metal foundries often release toxic pollutants such as arsenic into the atmosphere.

Water is also heavily polluted in many areas. Pollution in El Salvador is particularly bad and 90% of all the rivers are contaminated by chemical waste. In Honduras, Lago de Yojoa, the country's largest source of freshwater, has become polluted with heavy metals from the mining industry.

Soil erosion is also a major problem. For example, in Panama 50% of the soils are poor and 75% of the agricultural land is

Lorries carry away logs that have been illegally taken from forests in Darién, Panama. Although many areas of Central America are protected, illegal logging still occurs.

located on steep hillsides, which encourages soil erosion. In El Salvador, over 66% of all farm land suffers from soil erosion. Soil erosion not only impoverishes the agricultural land but causes major rivers and hydro-electric power stations to silt up. The Panama Canal is gradually being silted up because 70% of the forests along its banks have already been cut down, allowing the soil to wash away.

The coastal fringes of the region are also under threat. The mangrove forests are rapidly disappearing to make way for new settlements, tourist resorts and shrimp farms. Many commercial fish species breed in mangrove areas and their disappearance, combined with overfishing, could spell disaster for the coastal fisheries in the next decade.

Other marine areas, like the shallow waters off the coast of Nicaragua, are rich

▶ *Jaguars are present in all the countries of Central America and are the largest CARNIVORES in the region.*

◀ *The barrier reef of Belize is home to thousands of species of marine organisms. This is the blue hole on the Lighthouse Reef, which was formed when the roof of an underground cave collapsed.*

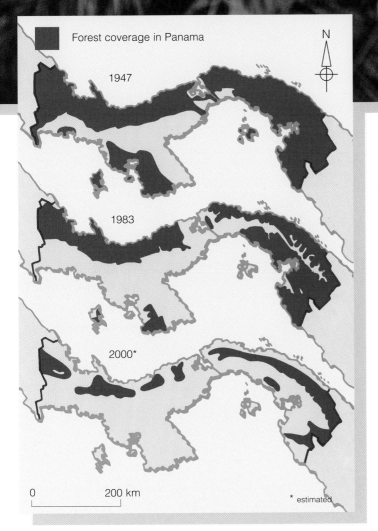

Forest coverage in Panama

1947

1983

2000*

N

0   200 km

* estimated

in rare species such as sea turtles. Belize has one of the finest coral reefs in the world, but the uncontrolled dumping of sewage into the Caribbean Sea is causing the waters to become degraded.

There are many positive initiatives that are being undertaken to help protect the environment. At a government level, for example, Panama has given protected status to 17% of its land area. Many people are aware of the environmental problems facing all seven countries and are campaigning to reduce pollution and protect areas of special biological importance. Community action, environmental education and the continuing traditional, sustainable land-use in Indian areas are all helping to confront the environmental problems facing the people of Central America.

THE FUTURE

There are many problems that need to be addressed before the lives of ordinary people can begin to improve in Central America.

As the population of the region is likely to double in the next 30 years, there will be more pressure to convert natural forest and scrubland into land for agriculture. The forest loss in the region so far has already caused local climates to change and increased the rate of soil erosion. Both these changes will affect the ability of each country to produce sufficient food for itself.

To provide additional employment, the nations of Central America are pursuing a policy of expanding their industrial capacity. But this too can have negative effects on the population. For example, 90% of El Salvador's rivers are contaminated with chemicals, and this is causing health problems. However, many countries are promoting the expansion of service industries, such as tourism and banking

▼ *Visitors in the Volcan Poás National Park in Costa Rica. Costa Rica is one of the countries interested in protecting wilderness areas and encouraging the development of the tourist industry to provide future employment.*

Some of the worst problems facing the region are drug trafficking, large scale destruction of natural forests, poverty and hunger, air and water pollution, and rapidly growing population. In all Central American countries, the wealth of the nation is concentrated in the hands of a small proportion of the population. The region has some of the poorest countries in the western hemisphere and has been ravaged by wars and civil wars for the last half a century. The 1990s, however, have ushered in a period of relative peace, and all seven countries have returned to democratic government. If peace can be maintained, then there is a possibility that the countries of Central America can create a brighter future for themselves.

▲ *The Cuna Indians of Panama have a legal title to their traditional land and also have elected representatives to try to help safeguard their future.*

which cause fewer environmental problems.

All the countries in the region have improved their education and health services over the last twenty years. Moreover, life expectancy throughout the region is higher than it was a decade ago and the number of people who can read and write is also increasing steadily. A healthier and better educated population will contribute more to developing the economy, by their ability to fill skilled job vacancies and by putting increased energy into their work.

KEY FACTS

● The poorest 20% of Panama's population only receive 2% of the national income while the wealthiest 5% receive 18%.
● Half the population of El Salvador does not have access to clean water.
● Belize has one teacher for every 25 students.
● In 1994, 57.9% of the population of Tegucigalpa, the capital of Honduras, were below the poverty line.
● Nicaragua is estimated to have 3.8 million ounces of unmined gold.
● The toll receipts from ships using the Panama Canal rose to US$ 463 million in 1995.
● Income from tourists visiting Costa Rica more than doubled from US$ 275 million in 1990 to US$ 661 million in 1995.

FURTHER INFORMATION

● BELIZE HIGH COMMISSION,
Harcourt House, 19 Cavendish Square, London W1
Provides information on Belize.
● EMBASSY OF COSTA RICA,
Flat 1, 14 Lancaster Gate, London W2
Provides information on Costa Rica.
● EMBASSY OF EL SALVADOR, Tennyson
House, 159 Great Portland Street, London WI
Provides information on El Salvador.
● EMBASSY OF THE REPUBLIC OF GUATEMALA,
13 Fawcett Street, London SW10
Provides information on Guatemala.
● EMBASSY OF HONDURAS,
115 Gloucester Place, London W1
Provides information on Honduras.
● NICARAGUAN HIGH COMMISSION,

8 Gloucester Road, London SW7
Provides information on Nicaragua.
● EMBASSY OF PANAMA,
40 Hertford Street, London W1
Provides information on Panama.

BOOKS ABOUT THE REGION
A Family from Guatemala, Julia Waterlow,
Wayland 1997 (age 6+)
Wayland Atlas of Threatened Cultures, Wayland
1996 (age 7–14)
*The People Atlas – People and Cultures around
the World,* Dr Brunetto Chiarelli and Lisa Anna
Bebi, Macdonald Young Books 1997 (age 10+)
Atlas of the Rainforests, Anna Lewington,
Wayland 1997 (age 7–14)

GLOSSARY

AMERINDIANS
The Indians of the Americas.

BIODIVERSITY
A word short for biological diversity, which means all the different plants and animals found in a particular area.

CARNIVORES
Mammals that are mainly meat-eating.

CHICLERO
A person that collects chicle from the rainforest.

CONTRAS
The rebel army that fought against the Sandinistas in Nicaragua at the end of the 1980s.

DEFORESTATION
The clearance of trees, for use as fuel or timber, or in order that the land can be used for a different purpose such as farming.

El NIÑO
A warm ocean current that, once every five to ten years, replaces the normally cold Pacific current off the coast of South America. This causes dramatic changes to the weather in Central America, bringing droughts or floods.

HYDRO-ELECTRICITY
Electricity produced when flowing water drives a generator.

GEOTHERMAL ENERGY
Heat obtained from geological activity deep in the earth which can be used to heat water to produce electricity.

GROSS DOMESTIC PRODUCT (GDP)
The total value of all the goods and services produced by a country, apart from money earned from investments abroad.

INDIGENOUS
The original inhabitants of a particular region.

ISTHMUS
A narrow piece of land connecting two larger areas of land.

MILPA
A farming system that was developed by the Mayas. The various staple food crops are planted side-by-side on small land holdings.

MONTANE
A word used to describe the climate or vegetation of mountain areas.

NORTHERN HEMISPHERE
That part of the world which lies to the north of the Equator.

SOIL EROSION
A process whereby soil is worn away by the action of the wind or by water.

TEMPERATE
A word used to describe a mild or moderate climate.

TORTILLAS
Round flat maize cakes.

TROPICAL
A word that is used to describe a climate that is characterized by high temperatures and rainfall.